MANDALA
COLORING BOOK

MANDALA
COLORING BOOK
Fabulous images to free your mind

SIRIUS

SIRIUS

This edition published in 2021 by Sirius Publishing, a division of
Arcturus Publishing Limited,
26/27 Bickels Yard, 151–153 Bermondsey Street,
London SE1 3HA

ISBN: 978-1-3988-1266-6
CH005749NT

Printed in China

MIX
Paper from
responsible sources
FSC® C016973

Introduction

This book contains a collection of lovely mandala outlines ready for you to color in and make your own. Mandalas are spiritual symbols which represent universal wholeness and balance. Found in many cultures, they are used for performing sacred rites and as instruments for mindfulness and meditation.

Drawing and coloring mandalas has long been thought to have a therapeutic effect. Finding a quiet moment to focus on this activity helps to calm and free the mind and encourages instinctive self-expression.

The mandalas included here offer a modern interpretation of the familiar symbol, using abstract graphics and images from the natural world to create the swirling shapes. All you need to complete them is your imagination and a set of colored pens or pencils.